Original title:
Island Hues

Copyright © 2025 Creative Arts Management OÜ
All rights reserved.

Author: Rosalie Bradford
ISBN HARDBACK: 978-1-80581-661-4
ISBN PAPERBACK: 978-1-80581-188-6
ISBN EBOOK: 978-1-80581-661-4

Sunlit Secrets and Lunar Hues

The sun forgot its glasses today,
It painted everything bright and gay.
A crab wore a hat, quirky and tall,
While seaweed danced, having a ball.

The fish threw a party, loud and proud,
With clam shell snacks, they attracted a crowd.
Seagulls told jokes, oh what a sight,
As the sandy beach giggled with delight.

Rocky Coasts Dressed in Palettes

Rocks in stripes, just like a suit,
They strutted around, what a hoot!
A starfish posed like it owned the shore,
While barnacles giggled and wanted more.

The waves tried to dance, but stumbled a bit,
Krabs cheered them on, "Just don't quit!"
Under the sun, with colors ablaze,
Even the sea foam joined in the craze.

Colors of a Hidden Paradise

In a hidden nook where laughter spills,
Parrots wear socks, now how do they feel?
A turtle in sunglasses sipped some juice,
Declaring, "Life's better with a little caboose!"

The sands whispered secrets, oh what a buzz,
As the gulls played bingo without any fuss.
A palm tree jived, in its own funny way,
Proclaiming, "Join in, it's a holiday!"

Shimmering Tides at Noonday

Tides sparkled like diamonds in the sun,
A fish in a tutu declared it was fun.
The beach ball bounced, full of glee,
Yelling, "Let's have a beach jamboree!"

A dolphin did flips, oh what a show,
While crabs formed a band, ready to go.
As the sun danced high, laughter did bloom,
The shoreline celebrated, dispelling all gloom.

Hues of Mirage and Memory

The sun wore sunglasses, too bright to see,
With lobster-red laughter, a sight so free.
Palm trees in the breeze danced like old goats,
While seagulls ordered fries and told bad jokes.

Fishes wore bow ties in the coral ball,
While jellyfish waltzed with no care at all.
A crab on a surfboard, what a weird sight,
As the tide slowly whispered, 'Let's party tonight!'

Waves of Color in Quietude

A rainbow flipped-flopped into the blue,
Thoughts of fruit salad in the midday hue.
Shells laughed in whispers, but I couldn't hear,
Too busy panicking when a wave drew near.

Bubbles like laughter played tag on the shore,
As I tripped over flip-flops, eyes wide, wanting more.
Starfish meditated, giving advice on peace,
While seaweed swayed like it couldn't be leased.

Dappled Shadows on Sandy Paths

Footprints on the beach in a wobbly line,
Wiggles and giggles, 'Was that line really mine?'
Turtles in sun hats rolled by with flair,
While clams threw a party without a care.

Sandy pies baked with a sprinkle of fun,
While crabs shared gossip under the sun.
The sun slipped a pancake across the blue sky,
And laughter erupted with a sweet lullaby.

The Song of Cerulean Seas

A fish in a tux made waves with each flap,
While dolphins critiqued my sunbathing nap.
The sea sang a tune of giggles and cheer,
While barnacles joined in, not one held a sneer.

A pelican juggled his lunch with finesse,
As sea cucumbers shared secrets, no less.
Bright umbrellas danced, kissed by the breeze,
In a world so absurd, laughter is the key.

Lush Retreats of Tranquility

In a hammock swaying, I snore,
The coconut falls, a surprise on the floor.
Lizards gossip, they plot and they scheme,
While parrots toss in a sunbeam.

With drinks so cold, they could swim away,
I sip and laugh through the sunny day.
The palms are dancing with style and grace,
But the wind just stole my fruity embrace.

A Symphony of Tides

The waves play music, a cheeky tune,
Sea foam giggles 'neath the bright, bold moon.
The crabs conduct with their tiny claws,
While fish make faces—what a great cause!

I join the dance, but trip on the sand,
The seagulls cackle, it's their own band.
A turtle winks with a sly little grin,
While I tumble again, it's just where I've been!

The Beckoning Blue

Oh, the sea is calling, I swear it's a hoot,
The fish are teasing, wearing hats quite cute.
Mermaids giggle as they splash all around,
Their fishy laughter is a bubbly sound.

I dive in hoping to join the parade,
But I forgot my floaties—oh what a charade!
The dolphins laugh as I flail and splash,
And I swear I swam faster than any old crash!

Golden Sands and Coral Winds

The beach is golden, a treasure so bright,
Sunbathers snooze, unaware of their plight.
I bury my friend in a sand castle grand,
But seagulls swoop down—now it's my hand!

A flick of the waves brings laughter and cheer,
As sand crabs scurry, oh dear, oh dear!
We chase the shadows, of jellyfish flights,
Summer's a playground of endless delights.

Tidal Brushstrokes

Waves paint the sand with glee,
Crabs tap dance, wild and free.
A flip-flop lost, it starts to roam,
Seagulls laugh at its new home.

Palm trees sway, joke in the breeze,
Bikini-clad folks dodge the bees.
With coconut drinks in hand, we cheer,
Sipping sunshine, what a dear!

Sunsets wink in colors bright,
Fish in shades of pink take flight.
Splashing giggles, a wild delight,
Nature's party each night!

Beneath the stars, we set our sights,
Lizards gossip about the nights.
As the tide rolls back with flair,
Funny things happen everywhere!

Whispers of the Coral

Beneath the waves, they softly chat,
Colorful fish wear tiny hats.
An octopus tells tales so bold,
While sea turtles nap, not a care to hold.

Starfish giggle, drifting about,
Playing tag with a sneaky trout.
The seaweed waves with a grin,
Making mischief beneath the din.

Bubble-blowers, blowing spheres,
Squeaky voices in my ears.
They swim around with much ado,
Creating laughter just for you!

Coral castles made of light,
Mermaids dance, oh what a sight!
The ocean's whispers tease and play,
Join the parade of sea's ballet!

Sun-Kissed Shores

On sun-kissed sands, we tumble and roll,
With jellyfish dreams, we lose control.
Tanned toes tangle in sun's warm blinks,
Slipping on water, our laughter sinks.

Kids build castles, grand and tall,
A wave comes crashing, down they fall.
"Let's add some moats!" they all declare,
Then laugh as sea foam turns their hair!

Picnic ants join with crumbs in tow,
As we chase seagulls putting on a show.
The sun gives a wink, with shades so bright,
We toast the day with sheer delight!

Evening wraps, the tides retreat,
We dance on shores with sandy feet.
Each grain a giggle, a joyful cheer,
Under the stars, no worries here!

Azure Dreams Unfold

In skies so blue, we spread our dreams,
With kite-fish flying, bursting seams.
A dolphin winks, a playful tease,
While others tumble in the breeze.

Sandy toes tell tales of fun,
"Catch me, catch me!" shouts the sun.
From flip-flops flung to hats that soar,
Crazy moments, who could ask for more?

Palm fronds rustle with whispered jokes,
While crabs in tuxedos make endless pokes.
The ocean's brush paints joy all around,
As laughter echoes, a blissful sound.

As twilight sets, the fireflies twirl,
With sparkles dancing like a whirl.
In azure land where silliness reigns,
Funny stories linger, that's how life gains!

Drenched in Color and Light

With suns so bright, I wear my shades,
A lobster's hue in sunny parades.
My nose, it gleams like a traffic light,
As seagulls laugh, what a silly sight!

The ocean splashes, my drink goes down,
A coconut hat makes me the clown.
Dancing crabs join the conga line,
With goofy moves, they steal the shine!

Rainbows sprout from my sassy shorts,
While fish nibble on my beachy worts.
Each splash a giggle, each wave a cheer,
Oh, the ocean's jest, all worries disappear!

So here's to laughter, sun, and fun,
Under a sky where craziness runs.
Hold your drink tight, and let's not fight,
This beach bum life is pure delight!

The Mirage of Tranquil Waters

Reflections shimmer, my hat's on tight,
Squinting hard, is that a fish or flight?
They swim like pros, while I just flop,
Regretting my leap to the boat's top!

Nearby, a turtle takes a nap,
While I try to dance and make a clap.
The ocean whispers, so soft and low,
"Please stop that jig; just go with the flow!"

A dolphin surfed in with a smirk,
I hollered, "Buddy, you're the real jerk!"
But laughter echoes, we join the spree,
Forget my flops; it's fun to be free!

So here's to mirages, both silly and bright,
Mixing good vibes, it's pure delight.
In waters calm, where giggles get caught,
Adventures await, and laughers are sought!

Secret Shades in the Breeze

A sun hat whispers, "Let's play a game,"
With colors so wild, it's never the same.
The palm trees sway, they're in on the joke,
While I try to charm a sunburnt bloke!

With shades in hues of banana and lime,
My laugh is contagious, like fish in crime.
The ocean dances, joining our crew,
While sneaky crabs hold a lawsuit too!

Beach towels fly, as kites in the air,
Jellyfish float like they haven't a care.
We groove to the rhythm of waves lunchtime,
Sandcastles rise like cities of rhyme!

So here's to secrets the breeze can unfold,
With laughter as bright as treasures of gold.
In summer's embrace, let's be genuine,
For fun's the best color, let it be our skin!

Harmonies of Green and Gold

In a field where grass is thick,
A goat wearing shades gives a wink.
He munches on leaves with a style,
Turning every head with a smile.

A parrot sings tunes in the air,
Hiding secrets, with flair and care.
The daisies dance in the bright sun,
While frogs jump around just for fun.

A lizard sunbathes on a rock,
Pointing at ants with a tick-tock.
The flowers laugh, they can't get enough,
In this place where all's just a bit rough.

So come join the ruckus, my friend,
Let's create mirth that won't ever end.
In colors so vivid and bold,
Life here is a canvas adorned in gold.

Dreaming in Ocean's Tints

A fish in a suit takes a stroll,
Thinking he's the star of the shoal.
With every flip, he waves hello,
In a sea of dreams, he's the show.

A crab with a cap on his head,
Dances around like he's been fed.
He claps to the beat of the tide,
While seaweed friends dance by his side.

The jellyfish float, what a sight,
With their glow, they light up the night.
And dolphins leap, so full of glee,
In this watery world, wild and free.

So dive into fun, take the plunge,
With creatures that giggle, dance, and lunge.
In hues so bright, they spin and prance,
Creating a party, a vibrant dance.

Sunlight on Turquoise Waves

A sunbeam winks on the rippling foam,
Where seagulls plot for a morsel or two.
They squawk and twirl; it's their fun home,
Nestled in laughter, the sky so blue.

A surfer spills, having quite the tumble,
Splashing like seaweed in a jolly mix.
He bounces back up with a chuckle, humble,
Ready to ride waves and perfect his tricks.

The sandcastle stands with a floppy hat,
While crabs gather round for a courtly meeting.
They argue and pinche on a mat,
Deciding who's best at pinching and eating.

In this place where giggles unfold,
With shades of colors, bright and bold.
So bring your beach chair, it's time to play,
In a world of fun, let's laugh the day away!

The Natural Canvas of Coastlines

On the shore where the splashes collide,
A turtle swims wearing a cool tie.
He's looking sharp, with pride as his guide,
In a world where the waves never lie.

A clam pulls a prank on a nearby snail,
With a joke that sends everyone reeling.
They laugh till they turn bright in the pale,
In this art piece, it's all about feeling.

The footprints in sand tell tales anew,
Of a crab that danced with a sea star.
Their funny cha-cha made quite the view,
As everyone cheered for the pair from afar.

So grab your palette, come join the show,
Artistry thrives where the tides ebb and flow.
In every splash, every break, every cheer,
Lies a canvas that welcomes all who come near.

The Dance of Sunset Colors

The sky giggles in pinks and gold,
As day bids night, brave and bold.
Clouds wear sombreros, bright and wide,
While the sun winks, then sneaks to hide.

A bubble floats, just out of reach,
Chasing colors, it starts to teach.
Dancing with dolphins, round and round,
In this twilight shop, joy is found.

The stars laugh as they take their place,
With twinkling eyes, they start to race.
Each hue is a jester, bright and spry,
Painting the horizon, oh my, oh my!

So let us twirl in merry delight,
Through this kaleidoscope, day turns night.
With giggles and grins, we celebrate,
This grand ballet the skies create.

Palms Waving in Technicolor

Palms in party hats, oh what a sight,
Waving wildly with pure delight.
They dance to the rhythm of the sandy shore,
Telling tall tales, who could want more?

Coconuts giggle, full of zest,
Joining the breeze in its playful quest.
Swaying like dancers in a comical ballet,
Shouting, 'Come join us, hip hip hooray!'

The sun throws confetti, a shimmering blaze,
As playful shadows join in the craze.
Each gust of wind adds to the fun,
It's a colorful fiesta under the sun.

So here we gather, on this merry patch,
With palms and coconuts, we'll all make a patch.
Laughing and spinning, let worries disperse,
In this carnival of colors, we all immerse.

Ocean's Whispered Tints

The ocean giggles, a cheeky tease,
With aqua whispers and playful breeze.
Spraying shades of frolic and fun,
As seagulls chatter, 'Watch us run!'

Waves wear their best cobalt dress,
Belly-flopping laughter, oh what a mess!
With every crest, a splash of cheer,
Even shells chuckle when they hear.

A crab moonwalks, with a sassy flair,
While flip-flops dance without a care.
Tides tickle toes, calling them near,
Join the blue parade, oh never fear!

So let's dip our toes in this liquid jest,
Ride the waves, and let hearts rest.
With ocean's hues, our spirits fly,
In this playful realm, we laugh and sigh.

Cerulean Gifts of the Breeze

The breeze arrives with a grin so wide,
Bringing treasures from the ocean tide.
A feather floats, then steals a hat,
A conch-shell calls, 'Come chat with that!'

Laughing leaves, like whispers of glee,
Bump into flowers, a jolly spree.
Each petal sways, in vibrant cheer,
As colors giggle, gathering near.

The sun cheekily paints the world bright,
Turning everything into a delight.
With every gust, a new surprise,
As painted moments dance before our eyes.

Join the ballet of colors and sounds,
Where fun is found in playful bounds.
Our hearts grow light like balloons in the air,
In this cerulean party, all troubles rare.

Where Tropics Meet Twilight

In the dusk, the mango trees sway,
While coconuts play hide and seek,
A parrot pretends to sing ballet,
And crabs dance with two left feet.

Sunsets spill like paint so bright,
Laughter echoes in the breeze,
Fireflies flutter, a twinkling sight,
Even the tide comes in with ease.

Languid waves whisper silly dreams,
As fish wear hats and flip-flops too,
Drifting on currents of giggling streams,
While the ocean waves say, "Boo-hoo!"

A hammock swings, a sleepy beast,
While iguanas sip their tea,
In this land, fun never ceased,
Where all is funny as can be.

A Spectrum of Silhouettes

In the glow of a setting sun,
Palm trees dance their silly tango,
Shadows of flip-flops on the run,
Catch a conch shell in a banjo.

Sandy toes wear sunbaked crowns,
Crickets audition their best tunes,
Seagulls waddle through sweet towns,
Where beach balls float like balloons.

Sandcastles crowned with jolly flags,
The kids compete in giggling fits,
While laughter echoes in sweet snags,
The tide knows all their little tricks.

Even the surf seems to chuckle,
As surfers ride like they have wings,
Each wave a giggle, and every bubble,
Sings of joy in aquatic flings.

Seashells Wrapped in Pastels

Pastel skies brush the ocean wave,
Seashells gossip without a care,
Turtles giggle in a sunny rave,
As starfish twirl in beachside wear.

A picnic basket filled with cheese,
And ants throwing a wild parade,
Beneath the palms, all come to tease,
While sandpipers join the charade.

Marshmallow clouds drift on a spree,
With colors borrowed from candy bars,
While dolphins joke beneath the sea,
Flipping jokes just like their stars.

Children chase the sunset glow,
Racing crabs in silly hats,
As laughter churns like ocean's flow,
These pastel dreams hold no spats.

The Rhapsody of Rustling Leaves

In a breeze where the funny sounds hum,
Leaves crack jokes with the sway of trees,
Bamboo shoots in a comedic drum,
As monkeys join the rustling tease.

A toucan jokes, a colorful sight,
With feathers brighter than a rave,
Tickled by dusk, under fading light,
While nature has secrets it won't save.

Laughter mingles with whispers of flow,
As critters compete for the best laugh,
Swaying to rhythms only they know,
In this leafy land's aftermath.

With every rustle, the comic plays,
Creating tales of jubilant play,
The leaves recite in their quirky ways,
A symphony of fun at the end of day.

Lush Vistas of Color

On the shore, the crabs all prance,
In flip-flops, fish do their dance.
With shades so bright, a parrot squawks,
While sunburned tourists count their socks.

Palm trees sway, like they've had too much,
Coconuts drop with a gentle touch.
A pineapple floats, like a tiny boat,
While seagulls plot, they must be remote.

The azure sky throws a laughing grin,
While cows in grass play violin.
In the colors, life's a blur,
Like a tourist's kite, caught in a stir.

Every splotch tells a silly tale,
Of mermaids' hair and fish that sail.
So grab a brush and paint the scene,
Let the laughter flow, bright and keen.

The Quiet Canvas

A canvas stretched beneath the sun,
Where jellybeans are on the run.
The coconut dreams of being sweet,
While candy fish hop on their feet.

Palm fronds tickle the gentle breeze,
While flamingos strut with such unease.
The paintbrushes giggle in delight,
As shadows chase away the night.

Marshmallow clouds float by, so light,
Their fluffiness makes the seagulls bite.
A snicker of laughter fills the air,
As artists trip over their own flair.

Easels wobble, and colors run,
The scene a riot, just pure fun!
Let brushes dip in every hue,
In this silly dance of what we do!

Driftwood Dreams in Pastel

Driftwood smiles on sandy shores,
Playing tag with ocean roars.
A crab in sunglasses takes a break,
While fish wear hats, for goodness' sake!

The sunset giggles in warm pastels,
As surfboards squeak with playful yelps.
A dolphin jumps, wearing a bow,
Belly flops, oh what a show!

Seashells whisper their secrets Old,
Tales of mermaids, glittering gold.
The painting's bright, a clownish sight,
As an octopus twirls in sheer delight.

In the splashes of color, hear the cheer,
Even the conch shells shed a tear.
For laughter flows like waves on sand,
In this dreamy, pastel wonderland!

The Sun's Palette on the Water

Bottled sunshine spills on waves,
While lazy fish act like knaves.
The water glimmers with a wink,
As skippers blush and sailors shrink.

A rainbow surfboard rides on high,
With whispers of the seagulls' sigh.
In the distance, a big whale jumps,
Landing with a splash and grumpy thumps.

Paint pots tumble off the sails,
As jellyfish throw paddy tales.
A bright sun wears a cheeky grin,
While sailors dance, eager to swim.

From azure waves to mango skies,
Every hue elicits surprise.
In laughter's embrace, the colors swirl,
As joy and mischief brightly unfurl!

Twilight's Warm Embrace

The sun dips low, a golden tease,
As flip-flops dance on sandy knees.
Seagulls squawk in a silly race,
Wishing they had legs to keep pace.

Laughter echoes, a playful breeze,
With coconut drinks that aim to please.
Palm trees sway, a funny sight,
As shadows stretch in the fading light.

Sandy Mirage

Footprints lead to nowhere fast,
As jellyfish float, a curious cast.
Sandcastles crumble with a laugh,
While crabs march on, their own path.

Sticky ice cream drips like rain,
A race against squirrels, oh what a pain!
Beach towels flutter, they take flight,
Chasing seagulls feels just right.

Azure Horizons

The sky's a prankster, blue and bright,
With clouds that dance in pure delight.
A flip-flop lands on a sunburned toe,
It's a comedy show, don't you know?

Bubbles pop with a gleeful puff,
While sunscreen battles get a bit rough.
Kids shriek as a wave splashes near,
Turning giggles into joyful cheer.

Palette of the Sea

Brush strokes of laughter paint the shore,
As fish tease kids, 'Come catch me more!'
Bright beach balls bounce without a care,
While clowns in floats give a silly stare.

Sunset paints the sky a pastel hue,
As chickens stroll, all dressed in blue.
A hula dancer with a big grin,
Spins around, let the fun begin!

Sunlit Serenity

A flamingo wears shades at noon,
While a crab dances, sings a tune.
The sun's a ball of melted cheese,
And gulls all fight for a strong breeze.

The sand's a blanket, comfy, wide,
Where sunbathers stretch with all their pride.
A built sand castle, tall and grand,
Is rivaled by a kid's quick hand.

The waves come rushing, splashing play,
A dolphin pops up, shows off, hooray!
We toss our cares to the salty air,
With laughter echoing everywhere.

So join the fun, let worries flee,
Get sandy toes and feel so free.
In this bright world of colorful glee,
Where smiles float just like a jellyfish spree.

The Colors of Solitude

A parrot squawks in purple tones,
While a turtle hums on sunlit stones.
With pineapples wearing tiny hats,
And a neighbor's goat trying to chat.

The coconuts gather for tea,
Course they gossip so loudly!
The waves giggle as they splash,
Competing with a fish in a dash.

A lime-green crab waves his claws,
As a sea horse plays by the faux pause.
The breeze plays tricks, tickling folks,
And laughter blends with ocean pokes.

So grab a friend, leave cares ashore,
Join the fun, share jokes and more.
In this whimsical land, find delight,
Where solitude is a humorous flight.

Ocean's Brushstroke

Each wave's a brush, splashing art,
In colors bold, makes quite a part.
The sun paints gold on buttered toast,
As seagulls giggle, making the most.

The beach umbrella's gone astray,
Caught in a dance of the windy play.
Flipped like a pancake, it twirls so high,
While crabs all cheer, letting out a sigh.

Fish sport hats, thinking it's neat,
As dolphins tap dance with fancy feet.
With every splash, laughter ignites,
In a canvas bright, filled with delights.

So let the ocean's whimsy unfold,
In playful strokes of blue and gold.
Together we create our own cheer,
In this comedy of color here.

Emerald Trails at Dawn

The trails of green weave through the sand,
Where tourists trip, all unplanned.
A parrot's laugh is infectious joy,
As it steals a sandwich from a boy.

The sunrise bursts in a vibrant grin,
Nature laughs, tickling skin.
While flip-flops flop with every stride,
A crab scuttles, feeling pride.

The palm trees sway in a funky groove,
As we shimmy and laugh, find our move.
A sudden splash sends us yelping,
In this merry world, all's just melting.

So come explore this silly morn,
Where every face is cheerfully worn.
With emerald trails inviting fun,
Our funny escapades have just begun.

Warm Breezes and Warm Colors

The sun wore shades of lemon bright,
While waves did dance in sheer delight.
A crab in flip-flops, quite a sight,
Sipped coconut juice with all his might.

The palm trees swayed, they seemed to grin,
As seagulls tried to join the din.
A beach ball bounced, then flew like sin,
And landed right on Mr. Finn!

With laughter ringing, light and free,
A piña colada for the bee.
The toucans hooted, such a spree,
One stole my hat and then flew flee!

So gather 'round, my friends, my crew,
We'll paint the sky in every hue.
With jokes and jests, our fun ensues,
In this wild place where laughter brews.

Where the Sea Meets the Sky

The waves would giggle, splash and play,
While clouds all danced in bright array.
A fish flew by, with quite the sway,
It winked at me, then swam away.

A sunburnt dude in shades so large,
Tried surfing, made a crazy charge.
He flipped and flopped like a foam barrage,
And washed ashore like a rogue at large.

The jellyfish wore polka dots,
While starfish boogied in their spots.
I joined them too in silly knots,
And someone yelled, "Hey! Connect the dots!"

But when the sun began to set,
The colors bloomed, no place for fret.
So grab a drink and place your bet,
On who'll fall in the least, I'll bet!

Verdant Echoes of Solitude

In the jungle gym of leafy dreams,
A monkey swung on mindless schemes.
His laughter burst like bubbling creams,
As he tossed coconuts in beams.

A parrot squawked, "You've got no game!"
While frogs crooned tunes of quite the fame.
With every jump, they played the same,
Each lizard watching, gnawing claim.

A sloth looked on in sleepy cheer,
He grinned and said, "I'll get there, dear."
With each slow step, he drew near,
And won the race by night, not fear!

So in this green, let's play along,
With critters singing nature's song.
If you trip on roots, it won't be wrong,
For laughter's where we all belong.

The Glimmering Mirage

A sunbeam bounced on golden sand,
It tickled toes and waved its hand.
A dolphin wore a party band,
And danced around, so truly grand.

A sand castle stood, so tall, so proud,
With turrets made of shells, quite loud.
A crab in crown, he was endowed,
Declaring "I'm the king!" to the crowd.

Then came the tide, with playful tease,
It tickled fancy, brought a breeze.
The king yelled, "Help! Save me, please!"
But all he got was quite a freeze!

Yet as the moon began to rise,
The scene transformed to sweet surprise.
With every wink of starry skies,
We laughed until the croc quite sighs.

Harmony in Seaside Tranquility

Seagulls squawk in silly flight,
Chasing waves with sheer delight.
Sandcastles rise, then swiftly crumble,
As kids all giggle, hearts not humble.

Crabs in tuxedos scuttle by,
Waving claws, they seem to sigh.
In the sun, a dog's bright grin,
Plays a game where none can win.

Bright beach balls flying in a row,
Hoping they won't land below.
Sunburned noses, ice cream drips,
Summer's charm in funny quips.

Together we frolic, join our dance,
To the waves we gladly prance.
Laughter spills like lemonade,
In seaside fun, joy won't fade.

Saffron Skies at Dusk

The sun retreats in vibrant flare,
And tells the day to take a dare.
A parrot sings a cackle tune,
While crabs plot mischief by the moon.

Bikini tops that just won't stay,
Scream for help but dance anyway.
Flip-flops fly like frisbees fast,
Chasing sunsets that won't last.

A fire pit crackles, laughter blends,
As marshmallows fly from hapless friends.
Tall tales of fish that got away,
Grow taller with each sunset's sway.

Sandwiched stories, bites of fate,
Toasting bread, though it's too late.
Saffron snakes in scrappy skies,
While everyone eats prize-winning pies.

Vivid Tints of Faraway Coasts

Frogs in flip-flops hop around,
With wild antics, laughter resounds.
Colors splashed on surfboards bright,
Whirling wonders in the night.

Octopuses in paint-splashed hues,
Throwing parties, forming crews.
Each tentacle a brush in hand,
Creating chaos—so unplanned!

Sandy toes and piña coladas,
Life's a feast with tropical baladas.
Dancing crabs on wooden planks,
Remind us to remember pranks.

Currents swirl in silly glee,
Washing in all that's carefree.
Adventure haunts the shores we see,
In vivid dreams—let's make it three!

A Meditation in Blue

Waves that whisper, "Come play here,"
Blues and greens in pure veneer.
A dolphin grins, a splashy jest,
While seaweed sways in silly quest.

Clouds that drift like fluffed-up sheep,
Teasing sailors not to sleep.
In the wind, a hat takes flight,
Through the sky it swirls in flight.

Turtles wear their shells with pride,
As they wander, side by side.
A picnic spread with ants in tow,
Gives a chuckle with every blow.

Harmonies in tunes of waves,
Bring to life the funny braves.
A meditation, strange and true,
In shades of azure, we renew.

Rainbow Reflections in Calm Waters

Beneath the sun, a fish wore shades,
Dancing bubbles, in bright parades.
They giggled and splashed, with great delight,
While crabs in tuxedos joined the sight.

A banana boat was quite the laugh,
As tourists tried to calculate their path.
One took a leap, slipped with a squeak,
Flipped in the air, how funny they peeked!

Seagulls wore hats made of straw,
Sipping drinks, with a joyful guffaw.
They argued over who had the best dish,
A seaweed salad? What a funny wish!

Fishy jokes echoed across the tide,
As dolphins played, full of pure pride.
Each splash a punchline, laughter so bright,
In the calm waters, pure joy takes flight.

Ocean's Lattice of Light

Light sparkled as fish did prance,
Jellyfish twirled like they were in a dance.
An octopus juggled shells so grand,
While turtles giggled, beach-bum band.

Light rays flickered, a disco scene,
Making waves where the seaweed had been.
A jellyfish crowned a clam with flair,
Together they laughed in the salty air.

Crabs in sunglasses roamed the sand,
Renaming tides, how grand they planned!
"Let's call that one the 'Crabby Moon',
And soon we'll salsa, oh, what a tune!"

In the lattice, light bent with glee,
Making shadows that danced with ease.
Each ripple a giggle, the sea was a treat,
With laughter that echoed, a playful beat.

Tropical Whispers

Palm trees whispered jokes in the breeze,
While monkeys swung, doing as they please.
A parrot squawked, "You're looking a bit dim!",
While the sun set slow, a colorful whim.

A coconut fell with a funny thud,
Landing near a snoozing sea slug.
"Hey there, sleepyhead, come join the fun!"
But the slug just sighed, "I'll pass on the run!"

Laughter bubbled like soda-pop fizz,
As crabs conferred—what a raucous quiz!
They wondered aloud which dance was best,
While chasing their shadows, they took a rest.

With whispers of humor, the night took flight,
Under starlit skies, everything felt right.
The island chuckled, a playground so vast,
Where jokes were treasures, and smiles were cast!

Shades of a Solitary Shore

At the edge of the shore, where the sand meets sea,
A lone flip-flop laughed, "What's wrong with me?"
It searched for its pair as waves rolled by,
And seagulls squawked, "That's a funny guy!"

A lone beach ball bounced with a grin,
Pretending to be the center of spin.
It rolled alongside a crab and a shell,
Together they played, ringing laughter's bell.

Driftwood rehearsed for a big stage show,
While coconuts cheered, "You'll steal the show!"
A clam nearby sang a solo too,
It crooned out loud in a comical hue.

As the sun dipped low, the shore became bright,
With shadows that danced in the fading light.
"Let's toast to this giggle, beneath the pink sky,
Fun's not just for two, but for all who pry!"

Reflections in Serene Waters

A duck plays chess, what a sight,
Floating past with pure delight.
Laughter echoes, waves reply,
As fish debate the sunlit sky.

A crab creeps up in a tuxedo,
Claiming the title of sea's hero.
While snails wear hats, quite the affair,
Sipping cocktails in salty air.

The Essence of Citrus Skies

Lemons dance on waves so bright,
Swimming past in sheer delight.
Oranges giggle, try to sail,
As grapefruits tell a juicy tale.

Bananas throw a beachside bash,
Slip 'n slide—a fruity splash!
While limes compete in a silly race,
Rolling fast, they find their place.

Vibrant Echoes of Sand

Sandcastles wear crowns of glee,
As tides laugh, setting them free.
Seagulls gossip, on the prowl,
While clams chime in with a growl.

Turtles dance in their little vests,
Hosting parties, all the best.
Shells are shuffling, what a scene,
In a world that's bright and keen.

A Symphony of Seaglass

Shards of color, like a show,
Glass musicians put on a glow.
Green and blue in harmony,
Bouncing light and jiving free.

A bottle sings its tale of woe,
As jellyfish sway, putting on a show.
In this concert, all's a joke,
Even octopuses dance and stoke.

Chasing Dusk's Fragrance

The sun wears a silly hat,
While crabs dance in a goofy spat.
Seagulls chuckle, stealing fries,
As I chase the scent, oh my, surprise!

A coconut laughs, jealous of the breeze,
Twirling palm trees sway with ease.
A rainbow fish winks with a grin,
Inviting me to dive right in!

As day turns to night, I trip on a shell,
The ocean cackles, 'Oh, do tell!'
Rolling over, sand tickles my face,
In the twilight, I find my place.

With lanterns made of jellyfish glow,
Whispers of laughter start to flow.
Chasing dusk, I stumble on glee,
In this silly, seaside spree!

Coastal Echoes

The waves giggle, a bubbly spree,
'Come join us!' they call, 'Let's be free!'
With flip-flops flung in the air,
I trip on shells, unaware of my flair.

Seagulls squawk a comedic song,
While sunburned tourists try to dance along.
A sandcastle prince loses his crown,
As a wave sweeps him straight to town!

Sunshine beaming, my ice cream melts,
I chase it around, as laughter swells.
A crab scuttles, pinching a toe,
And suddenly, we're stealing the show!

Under the moon, shadows twist and play,
Funny whispers of the end of the day.
With each echo, a giggle finds me,
In coastal laughter, forever we'll be!

The Dawn's Gentle Caress

Morning yawns, rubbing its eyes,
Awakening to a world of surprise.
A fish in pajamas leaps with delight,
Waving to jellyfish, 'What a sight!'

Seashells gossip on the sandy shore,
"Who wore it better?" they ask, wanting more.
The sun, with a wink, claims its throne,
Casting tiny shadows, it's never alone.

The coffee's cold, but who cares?
I'm dodging seagulls in all my layers!
As dolphins perform leaps of pure joy,
I chuckle and cheer, it's a grand ploy!

With sunglasses stuck on my messy hair,
I stumble and trip without a care.
The dawn whispers gently, 'Oh, what a thrill!'
In morning's embrace, I'm taking my fill!

Sun-Kissed Reflections

The sun's a prankster on the sea,
Bouncing off waves, laughing at me.
With shades on my nose, I take a glide,
Tripping on flip-flops, oh what a ride!

The tide whispers tales, mixed up and fun,
About a crab who dreams of the sun.
As umbrellas bob like colorful boats,
I chat with a seagull, sharing our quotes.

My towel's a trampoline, bounces galore,
As I land with a splat—oh please, no more!
The sun, like a jester, rolls on the ground,
In laughter, I lay, feeling quite round.

Reflecting on moments, silly and bright,
With friends by my side, what a joyful sight!
With giggles and glimmers of sun on the sand,
We dance to the rhythm of joy, hand in hand!

Tides of Aquamarine Dreams

Waves giggle under the sun's bright grin,
Crabs dance like they're in a wild spin.
Seagulls squawk jokes with a silly twist,
While turtles practice salsa, they can't resist.

Pineapples sport shades, looking quite bold,
Jellyfish play games, their laughter untold.
Fish wear bow ties, swim with great flair,
Underwater parties, a splash everywhere.

Llamas in shades stroll the sandy shore,
Chasing the tide, then back for some more.
Each splish and splash brings smiles like candy,
As the sun sets over this world so dandy.

So here's to a place where silliness reigns,
Where laughter and bubbles wash off all pains.
In the tides of dreams, let's keep losing the fight,
For the fun never ends, under moonlight so bright.

Sunset Serenade

Crickets sing loudly, a chorus in the dusk,
While a dapper octopus smooths out his husk.
Guitar-fish jam on the coral stage,
In this sunset game, we've hit the right page.

The sun winks as it paints the sky pink,
While a pelican sips from a pineapple drink.
Squid flip pancakes from the ocean floor,
Giggling fish pass around bubble gum lore.

Laughter bubbles up like the tide's merry swirl,
As the day waltzes off, giving night a twirl.
Fireflies twinkle, echoing the smiles,
While everyone grooves in this land of guiles.

So raise your glass high, let's toast to this cheer,
In a world of fun, where silliness is here.
With friends all about and the sunset so grand,
Every moment we share, we dance hand in hand.

Secrets in Silken Sands

Beneath the soft grains, the whispers are loud,
As starfish declare they're feeling quite proud.
Clams spill the beans on who's making the fuss,
While snails carry secrets without any rush.

With buckets of laughter, we dig for delight,
As jellybeans tumble with all of their might.
A crab in a hat throws a party for two,
While clowns in the sea show their best jig or two.

Oh, the treasures we find in this playful parade,
From seashells to giggles, all perfectly laid.
With sea glass as jewels and laughter our tune,
We spin in the breeze, beneath the bright moon.

So gather your friends, let's build a grand fort,
With walls made of joy, it's the silliest sport.
In the secrets of sands, where fun never ends,
We'll cherish these moments with laughter, our friends.

Splash of Sunset Colors

The sun throws paint in a wild, bright jest,
While otters create chaos, they just can't rest.
With brush tails a-swirling, they conjure a scene,
Of rainbows and giggles, oh how they convene!

Crayons of coral and violet embrace,
As seahorses prance in an underwater race.
The jellyfish jive, a disco delight,
Where bumps and splashes make everything right.

Ocean's a canvas; it's swirling with glee,
As colors collide in pure jubilee.
While waves roll in, taking laughter away,
Each splash tells a story, come join in the play!

So join this parade of hues, bright and bold,
Where stories are told, and laughter unfolds.
In the splash of the moment, with every embrace,
Let's dive into joy, in this magical space.

Dunes and Dreams

In the sand, I found a shoe,
But it wasn't mine, just left for two.
I laughed aloud, such silly finds,
Like searching for gold in the world's odd kinds.

Seagulls squawk, they steal my fries,
With a glance that says, we're all big guys.
Waves crash down like playful pets,
Who knew the beach could inspire such bets?

The wind plays tricks, a playful tease,
My hat flew off, oh what a breeze!
It danced away, my hair a mess,
Who knew the ocean was life's big jest?

But I won't fret over sand in my toes,
Each grain's a memory, as the sun goes.
Tomorrow I'll chase, with waves as my guides,
In this land of laughter, where whimsy resides.

Nature's Ingenious Tapestry

Look at the trees, they sway and twirl,
As if they're all in a merry whirl.
The flowers giggle, in colors bright,
Creating a scene that feels just right.

The clouds above play hide and seek,
One's a dragon, the other a cheek!
The sun peeks through, a playful face,
As if it knows we're in this race.

Squirrels plot with acorn schemes,
While frogs croak loud, or so it seems.
Nature's quirks, a clever sigh,
In this tapestry, we laugh and cry.

With every breeze, a giggle's caught,
In a world where nothing's quite as thought.
So let's embrace their funny plots,
In nature's dance, we're all that we've got.

Rhythms of Kamala Sea

The waves beat out a silly tune,
As crabs perform, beneath the moon.
They scuttle left, then right, they jive,
In this sandy club, they come alive.

Surfboards wobble with strength unknown,
As I ride waves, I feel outgrown.
I tumble down with a splash and cheer,
The ocean laughs, its humor clear.

Shells whisper secrets, oh what a laugh,
Each a story, a bit of a gaffe.
The seaweed waves like a hand in jest,
In these rhythms, I find my rest.

I'll dance with dolphins, wiggle with glee,
With fish that snicker, oh, can't you see?
In the rhythms of laughter, we play our part,
In the Kamala sea, a joyful heart.

Kaleidoscope of Coastal Enchantment

Colors swirl like a paintbox spree,
With splashes of laughter, wild and free.
The beach umbrella tilts with grace,
As I chase down chips in a mad race!

The tide sneaks in, a cheeky thief,
Stealing my flip-flops, oh what a grief!
But every splash brings glee anew,
In this coastal charm, all worries flew.

Seashells whisper with gossip galore,
Like old friends sharing secrets on the shore.
The sun smiles down, a bright prankster,
As I sunbathe without a care, a true gangster!

With laughter echoing, the world feels light,
In this kaleidoscope, everything's bright.
So here on the coast, where whimsy blooms,
Let's take a bow for the sea's funny tunes!

Verdant Dreams Among the Waves

In the green of the palm, a monkey swings,
Chasing after dreams and silly things.
He slips on a coconut, lands with a thud,
Now he thinks he's a fish, oh what a dud!

The crabs in the sand wear tiny hats,
Dancing to tunes of the splashy spats.
A parrot squawks jokes, oh what a riot,
In this place of laughter, who wants to be quiet?

The sun overhead, throws glittering rays,
While jellyfish giggle in foamy ballet.
A turtle with shades glides by with a grin,
Saying, "Catch me if you can, I bet you can't win!"

With songs of the waves and humor aflame,
Life here is silly, but never the same.
In dreams of the sea, oh the fun we'll see,
Tomorrow let's wake with a laugh and a spree!

The Palette of Paradise

Paintbrushes of waves swirl colors so bright,
While seagulls dip down, a comical sight.
A crab wearing glasses reads all the laws,
Says, "No fighting in sand, we'll play without flaws!"

The fish in the rocks toss a party all night,
With disco balls made from shells, what a sight!
They spin and they twirl in their glittery best,
Even the clams say this is quite a fest.

A toucan drops juice from a tree's heavy bough,
The party spills laughter and thrills for the now.
With balloons made of seaweed, they float in the breeze,
As laughter erupts like the waves on the seas.

At sunset, they paint the horizon in cheer,
With tints of bright laughter that echo so clear.
In this colorful life, every joy, a surprise,
A festival of fun beneath widening skies!

Coral Embrace

In a coral castle, a clownfish resides,
Wearing a frown while the seahorse rides.
He says, 'Why so serious? Let's twirl with grace!'
And dances around with a big fishy face!

A starfish named Sam draws hearts in the sand,
While octopus artists create their own band.
With eight arms all waving to a bubbly beat,
They charm all the waves with their slippery feet.

"Life's too short," says a clam, "for whispers and sighs,
Let's throw a big bash and color the skies!"
So they gather the shells, the barnacles too,
For a funny fiesta beneath ocean blue.

In this ocean embrace, with joy that won't stop,
Even dolphins are laughing, spinning, and hop.
As fish wrapped in seaweed sway back to sea,
They'll always remember this goofy jubilee!

Cerulean Mornings

Dawn breaks with laughter and witty refrains,
As dolphins play tag 'round the rock with the canes.
The sun pops up like a big golden egg,
And a pelican jokes, "Let's stretch out a leg!"

The waves whisper secrets to sandcastles fine,
While crabs hold their court, drinking seaweed wine.
With shell phone in hand, they call up their friends,
To share all the giggles that morning extends.

A local sea turtle wears flip-flops with flair,
Skating on waves, what a sight to declare.
He says, "Join the ride, let's hold onto fun,
Before we get baked by this warming sun!"

As laughter erupts with each splash of delight,
Mornings here shimmer with comic insight.
In cerulean mornings where whimsy prevails,
Every tide is a chuckle that never grows stale!

Mosaic of the Forgotten Reef

Coral bows in vibrant sneers,
Fish are wearing tiny gears.
An octopus with inked tattoo,
Claims he's a pirate, but he's blue.

Starfish give the ocean a wave,
Sandy crabs are trying to behave.
Underwater parties shake and swirl,
As seaweed twirls in a playful whirl.

Jellyfish are floating with grand ease,
Dancing gracefully in ocean breeze.
Who knew that reefs had such a laugh?
Even shells are joining in the paph!

Bubbles rise like joy in air,
Fish are joking without a care.
In this deep, they play and hop,
Creating mischief that won't stop.

Paintbrush of the Setting Sun

The sun dips low with colors bold,
Its paintbrush spills hues of gold.
Silly shadows start to prance,
As gulls laugh in a feathered dance.

Clouds claim they're cotton candy fluff,
While waves play tag, calling each bluff.
Palm trees shimmy, shaking their fronds,
Sending coconuts for magical bonds.

The sky wears a gown of purple and pink,
While crabs joke about how to sync.
They hold concerts with rock and roll,
Even the dolphins start to stroll.

As twilight giggles, nightbirds croon,
It's a silly tune under the moon.
Where laughter swirls with the evening light,
Sprinkling joys till the morning bright.

Harboring Shades of Tranquility

A turtle cruises, slow and proud,
Waves are splashing, singing loud.
A parrot squawks with colorful flair,
While fishermen gossip without a care.

The pier creaks with each odd step,
Seagulls swoop, as if they prepped.
With nets in hand and dreams galore,
The fishermen laugh and share folklore.

Boats tilt like they're on a sway,
Wishing they could dance all day.
Crabs hold court, ruling the sand,
Their tiny claps, a cheering band.

With gentle breezes blowing around,
Tranquility's humor knows no bound.
Mist of salt adds a ticklish tease,
In this harbor, all hearts are at ease.

Ferns and Flamingo Fables

Ferns whisper secrets to the breeze,
Flamingos prance like they're at ease.
In a tale where colors collide,
Beaks and leaves take a silly ride.

"Why do you stand so tall and thin?"
Said the ferns with a gentle grin.
"Because I know how to strike a pose,
While you just sway where no one knows!"

Flamingos struck a funny pose,
Wiggling toes in flashy clothes.
They argue who got the brighter hue,
While ferns just laugh, feeling brand new.

Together they spin a whimsical yarn,
Of summer days and soft green dawn.
Their fables mingle with giggles bright,
Where ferns can dance and flamingos take flight.

Vibrant Selves beneath the Canopy

In a jungle of laughter, we dance around,
Swaying like coconuts that bounce on the ground.
With colors so bright, our spirits ignite,
We paint the whole scene with joy in a sight.

The monkey is laughing, it swings with a grin,
While crabs on the beach join the playful din.
We wear flower crowns, so silly, so bold,
Chasing after rainbows, not doing what we're told.

The parrot squawks secrets, oh what could it mean?
In a world of pure nonsense, we're reigning supreme.
Our vibrant selves flourish in shades so untamed,
Making memories wild, forever unframed.

Here's to the vibrant, the wacky, the free,
In a canopy laughing, come join us and see.
With every twist, turn, and giggle we share,
We thrive in this chaos, no worries, no care.

Secret Coves and Whispered Colors

In hidden little nooks where the sea meets the sand,
Shells giggle in whispers—can you understand?
The waves tell the jokes that the seagulls all hear,
While flip-flops are dancing, let's give them a cheer!

Under the palm trees, we're dodging the sun,
Playing peek-a-boo til the tide starts to run.
With colors of laughter painted over our cheeks,
We blend in with the sandcastles, giggling geeks.

A crab with a bowtie joins our beach parade,
While jellyfish jelly is drizzled and made.
The starfish is winking, it knows all the tricks,
Together we sparkle, our laughter so quick.

When twilight approaches, we sing to the breeze,
In secret coves splendid, we do as we please.
With whispers of colors in twilight's soft light,
We'll dance 'til the stars start to twinkle at night.

Mosaics of Sunsets

In a canvas of colors that change with a chuckle,
The sky is a jigsaw that's ready to snuggle.
With shades like a dessert, sweet orange and pear,
We giggle in hues, bursting forth in mid-air.

Pineapples tumble as we surf on the tide,
While splashes of fun are the waves we confide.
With bright fuchsia hats and surfboards so prime,
We ride on the giggles, no hurry, no time.

As the sun dips and winks, we play tricks on fate,
While colors collide in a whimsical state.
With laughter so loud that the seagulls all clap,
We're mosaics of sunsets—a colorful map.

Lets capture these moments, pixel by pixel,
In flip-flop conundrums, we twist and we tickle.
So toast to the colors that dance in our hearts,
As we create a spectacle, laughter in parts.

Vibrant Reveries by the Shoreline

On a snappy shore where the breezes frolic,
We spin in our dreams, oh so joyous and colloquial.
The sand tickles toes, we giggle with glee,
Count the jellybeans washed up by the sea!

A crab in a tux kicks up quite the fuss,
While dolphins are plotting a splashy new bus.
Each wave tells a story, in feta and cheese,
As we feast on the laughter carried in the breeze.

Our beachballs are bouncing like they have a life,
Competing for air against seagulls in strife.
With shades of bright summer like a candy delight,
We dance in the colors 'til day turns to night.

So join us, dear friend, in our vibrant parade,
In the symphony wild, where worries all fade.
With reveries bright, let's twirl 'round and sway,
At the shoreline of fun, we'll play all day!

www.ingramcontent.com/pod-product-compliance
Lightning Source LLC
Chambersburg PA
CBHW072129070526
44585CB00016B/1588